YES, I CAN HELP YOU WRITE A BOOK!

From Idea to Outline:
A Step-by-Step Workbook for
Aspiring Authors

By D. L. Armillei

First edition, February 2023
ISBN 978-1-7379179-1-5 [softcover]

Diamond Cove Publishing, LLC,
P.O. Box 2292, Palm Harbor, FL 34682-2292

Diamond Cove
Publishing

Greetings, fellow wielders of the written word!

Welcome to the enchanted realm of storytelling, where ideas are transformed into magic and words are woven into spells.

If you have a great tale simmering in your imagination and you're eager to cast its spell upon the page, but you're not quite sure where to start, have no fear. You're in good company among the many aspiring wizards of the written word.

But the good news is, with a little guidance and the right resources, anyone can conjure their vision into a well-crafted novel.

As an award-winning, international bestselling fantasy author and master of the art of storytelling, I understand the power of the written word and the challenges of harnessing that power to bring your tale to life.

I also know, as an author, the question I get asked most often is, "Can you help me write my book?" Lo and behold, I have arrived to disclose the truth - the answer is a resounding yes!

With a bit of guidance and a touch of magic, you can transform your idea into a spellbinding novel.

So, grab your quill and join me on a journey to outline your story ideas and unleash the magic of your imagination!

Donna

① GENRE

A book's genre refers to its category or classification based on shared characteristics, such as subject matter, style, and intended audience.

Each genre has different expectations of readers. For example, a mystery novel requires a clear puzzle to be solved, while a romance novel focuses on the relationship between the characters.

Understanding the genre helps you, as an author, meet readers' expectations and tailor the story to the target audience's preferences.

Some popular genres include romance, science fiction, fantasy, mystery, and horror.

Publishers specialize in specific genres, so knowing the target genre will help you find the right publisher.

Write your book's genre here:

_____

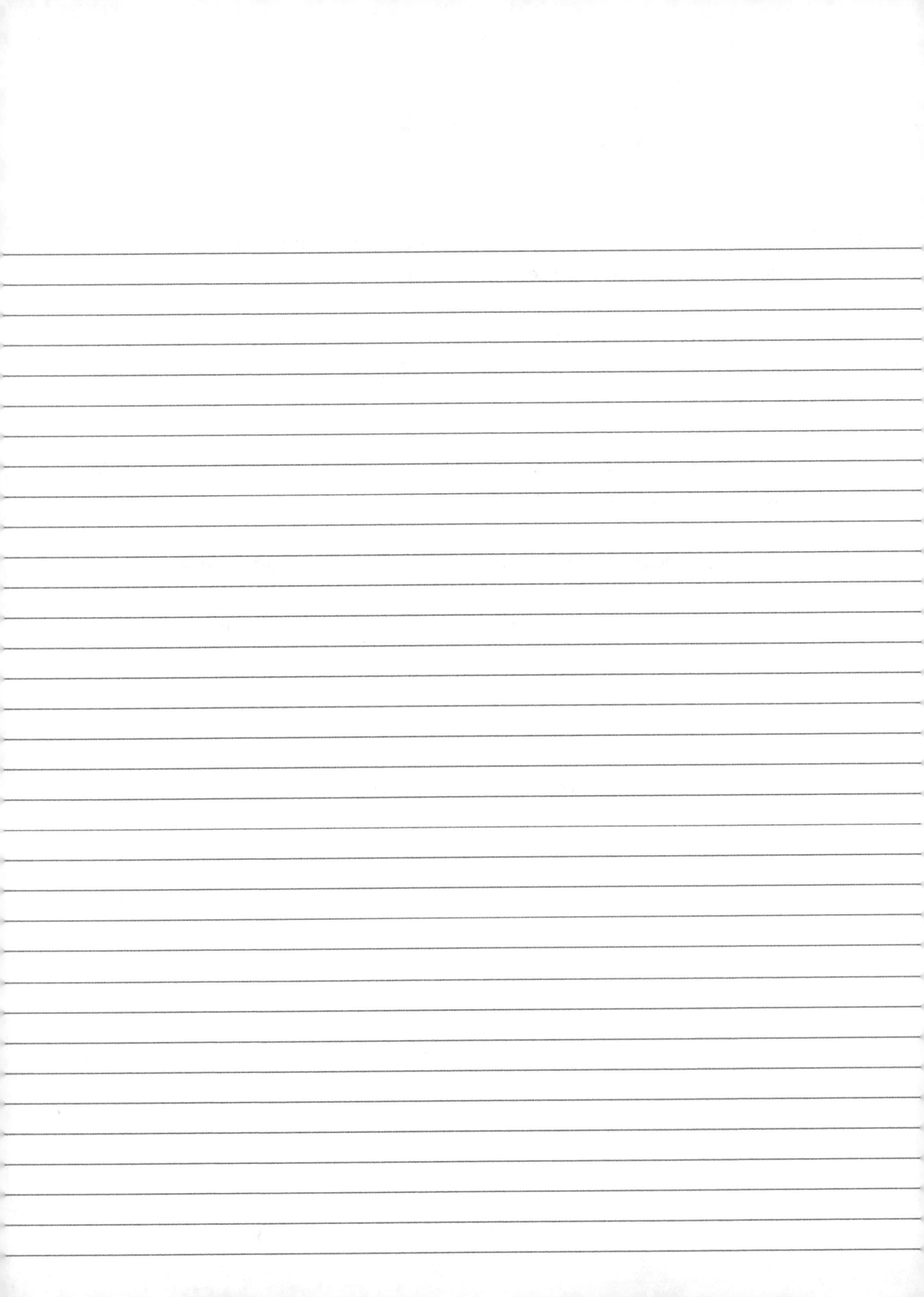

② THEME

A book's theme is the underlying message or meaning the author is trying to convey through the story.

It's the central idea that ties together the plot, characters, and setting.

The theme often explores universal truths and human experiences and can be interpreted in different ways by different readers.

Some common themes found in fiction are self-discovery, isolation, friendship, romance, power, grief, survival, forgiveness, social injustice, and the meaning of life.

Write a brief summary of your story idea (theme) below.

_____
_____
_____
_____
_____
_____
_____
_____
_____
_____
_____
_____
_____
_____
_____
_____
_____
_____
_____
_____

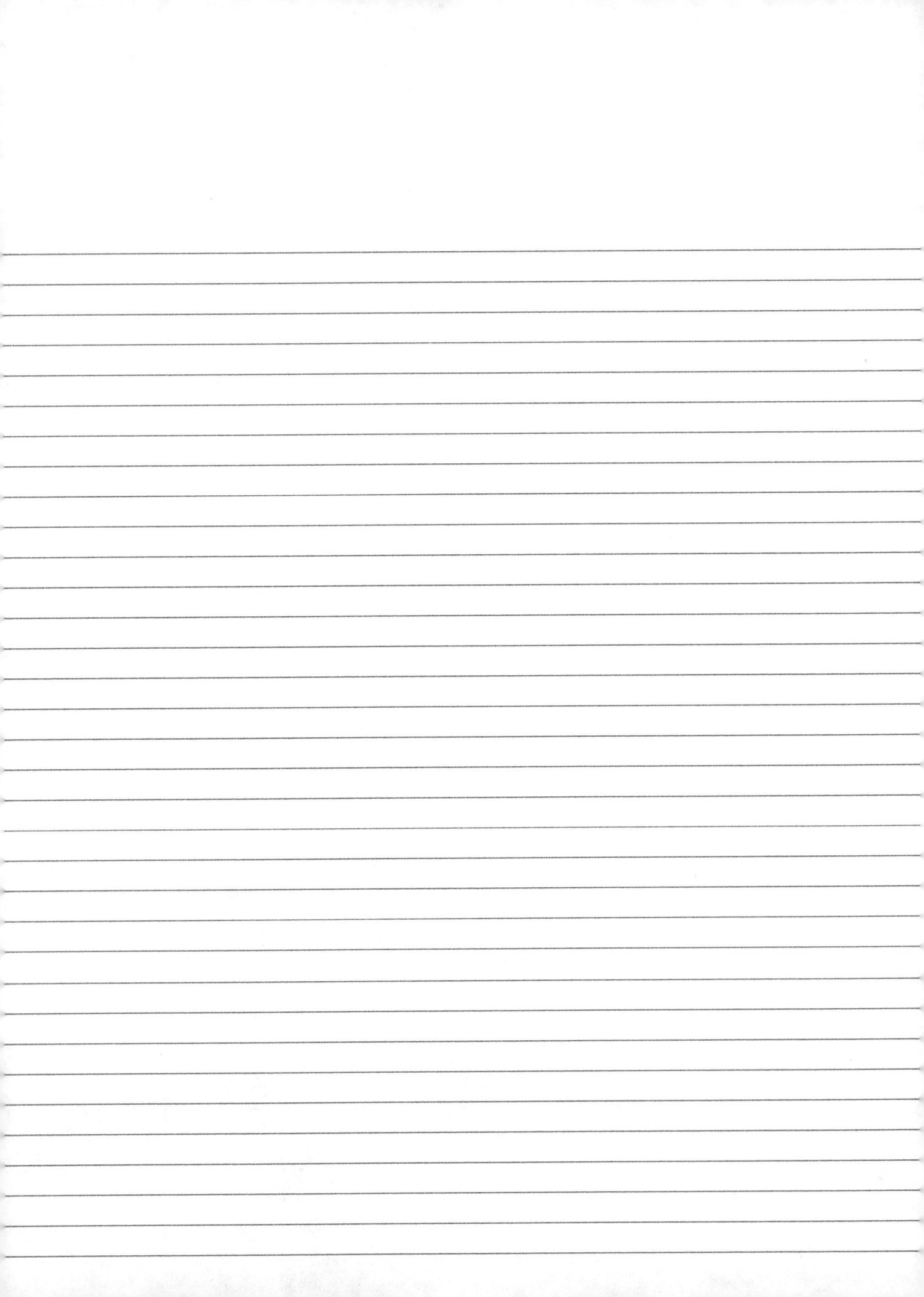

③ LOGLINE

A logline, also known as an elevator pitch, is a concise and compelling one or two-sentence summary of a book's premise that conveys the essence of the story in a clear and engaging way.

A strong logline is important because it's often the first thing a prospective reader or publisher will encounter, and it serves as a hook to draw them in and make them interested in reading further.

It can also help your book stand out from the crowd and generate buzz and excitement around your novel.

Crafting a logline for your book before writing it can help you stay focused on the central theme or idea you're trying to convey while ensuring all the elements of your story are working together to create a cohesive and captivating whole.

What's your book's logline?

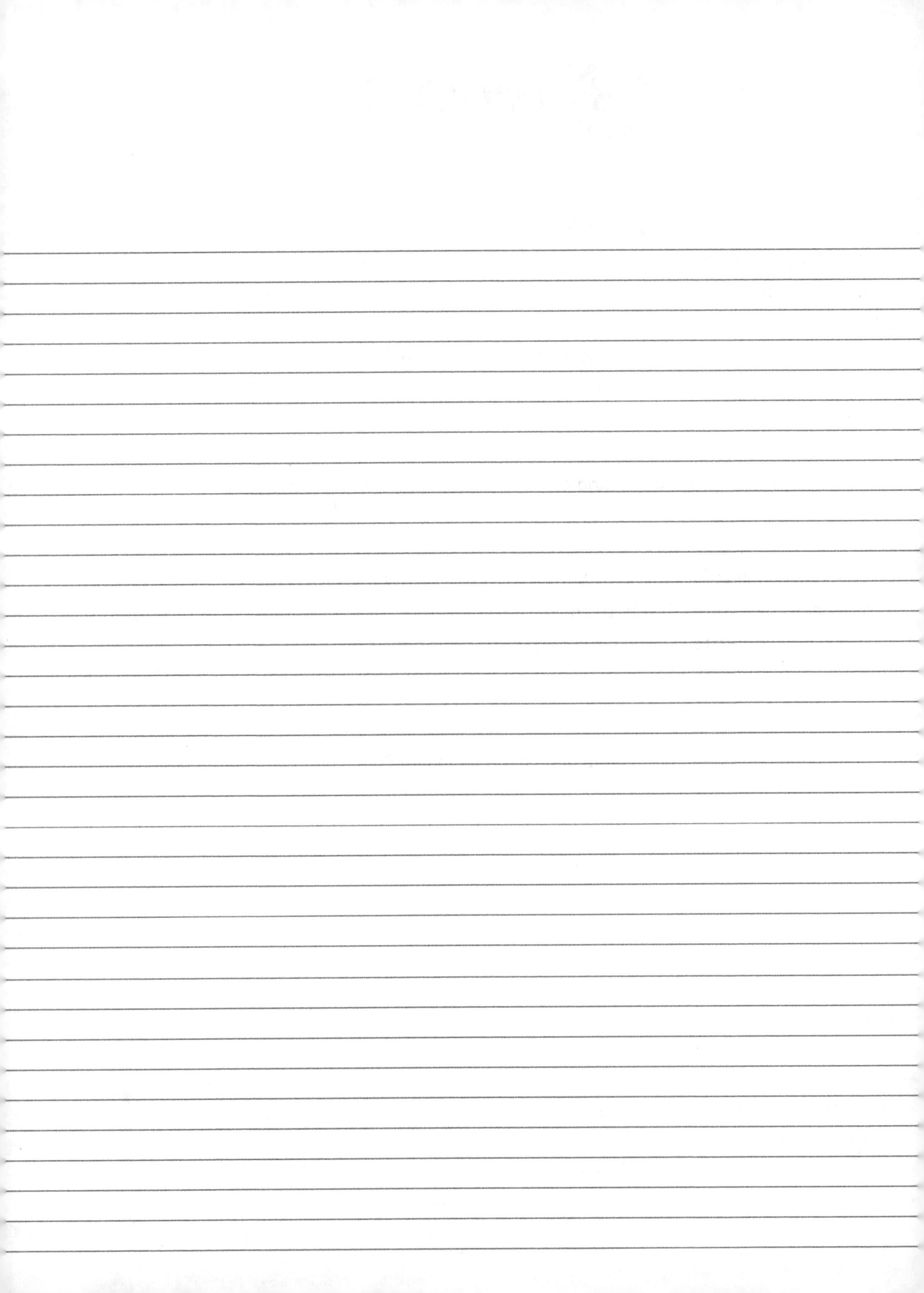

④ NARRATIVE VOICE

The narrative voice defines the perspective from which a story is told. It's how the author presents the events and characters in their story to the reader.

The narrative voice can be a first-person point of view, a third-person point of view, or an omniscient point of view.

In a first-person narrative voice, the story is told from the perspective of a character who is part of the story. The narrator uses the pronouns "I" and "we" to describe the events and characters.

In a third-person narrative voice, the story is told from an outside perspective, usually by a narrator who is not a character in the story. The narrator uses pronouns like "he," "she," and "they" to describe the events and characters.

In an omniscient narrative voice, the narrator is all-knowing and can access the thoughts and feelings of all the characters in the story. The narrator may also provide commentary or analysis of the events and characters.

The choice of narrative voice can have a significant impact on how a story is perceived by the reader. It can affect the level of intimacy, objectivity, or emotional connection the reader feels toward the characters and events.

What's your book's narrative voice?

_____

(5) SETTING

The setting in a story refers to the time and place where the story happens. It includes the physical location, cultural and historical context, and time period in which the events occur.

It's important because the setting provides the reader with a framework to imagine the story's events, characters, and actions. It helps establish the mood, atmosphere, and tone and can impact how the characters behave and interact with each other.

Some examples of settings used in fiction novels are urban, rural, fantasy, historical, science fiction, and domestic.

The setting plays a critical role in enhancing the reader's experience and immersing them in the story's world.

Where and when does your story take place?

_____
_____
_____
_____

What's the significance of this setting?

_____
_____
_____
_____

What mood or atmosphere do you want to create?

_____
_____
_____
_____

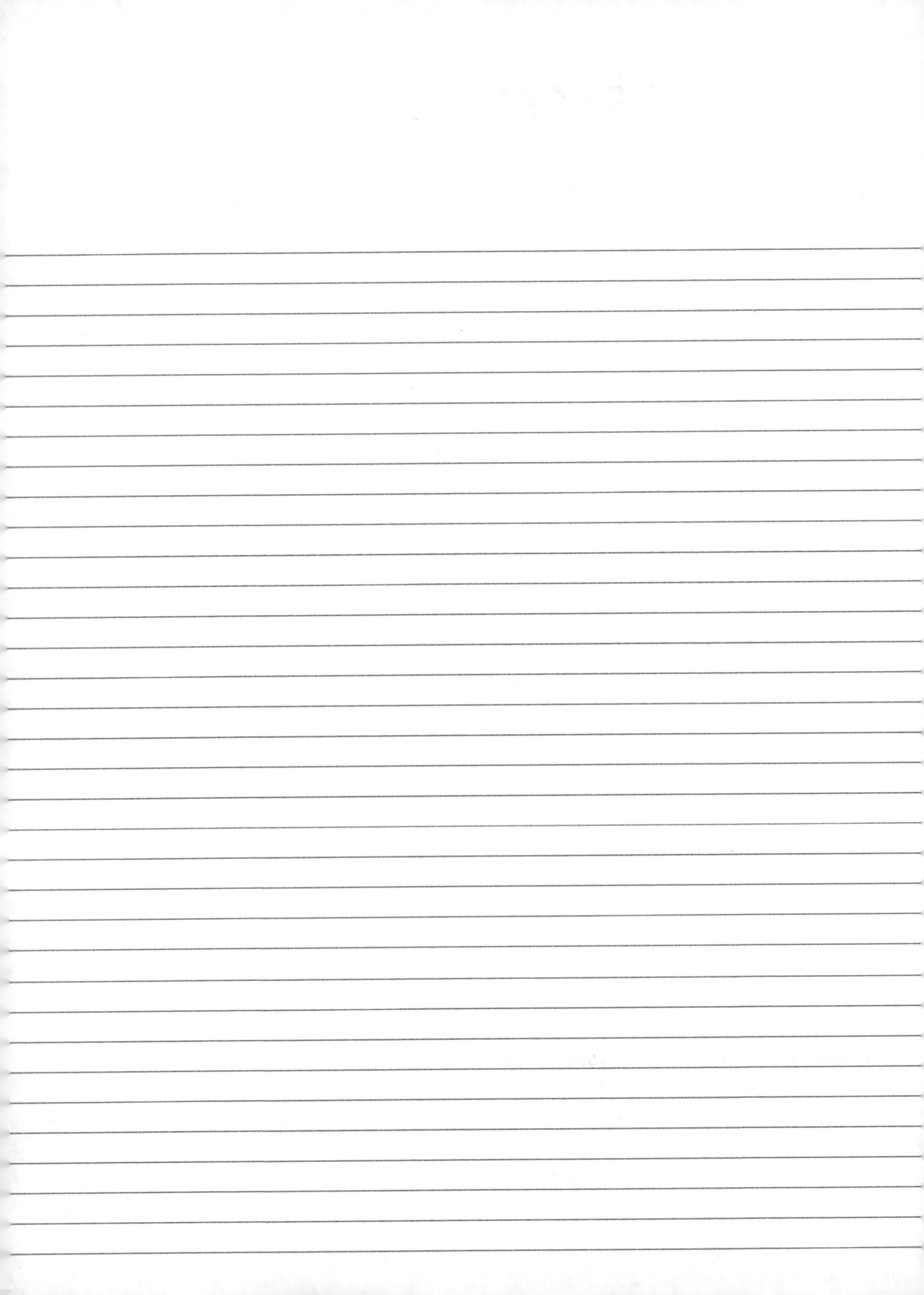

⑥ MAIN CHARACTER

The main character of a story, often called a protagonist, is the hero/heroine who drives the plot forward and faces the central conflict or challenge of the narrative. The story's narrative is the sequence of events, actions, and experiences that make up the plot and create a unified and meaningful tale.

The protagonist is the character the reader follows and empathizes with throughout the story.

It's important to create your protagonist using defining characteristics. These are the traits or qualities that distinguish your protagonist from other characters in the story, such as their personality, values, beliefs, strengths, weaknesses, or physical attributes. These characteristics shape the character's actions and decisions and help the reader understand and relate to them on a deeper level.

Answer the following questions to outline your main character's defining characteristics.

What's your main character's worldview?

_____
_____
_____
_____

What's one characterizing detail that shows their personality? Their quirks?

_____
_____
_____
_____

What makes your main character extraordinary?

_____
_____
_____
_____

⑦ MAIN CHARACTER
(continued)

What's your main character's attitude toward other people?

_____
_____
_____
_____

How do they dress? Speak?

_____
_____
_____
_____
_____

What makes your main character likable to the reader? They can be mean but must show a redeeming quality to get the reader to want to spend hours reading their story.

_____
_____
_____
_____
_____

What phrase characterizes your main character best?

It's good to know the excessive details about your main character, but the phrase you write here is usually all you'll use in the story. You'll convey the rest of the description through what the characters say and do.

For example, in the Harry Potter books, Harry Potter is described as "The Boy Who Lived", referencing his survival of the killing curse cast by the dark wizard Voldemort.

_____
_____

(8) MOTIVATION & GOAL

Knowing your protagonist's motivation and goal is essential for crafting a cohesive and well-structured story. It's what drives the narrative and creates tension and conflict that keeps readers interested in your book.

A character's motivation is the driving force behind their behavior or actions. It's what propels them forward, what they hope to achieve, or what they are trying to avoid.

On the other hand, a character's goal is a specific, measurable, and time-bound objective they strive to accomplish.

An example of a character's motivation may be a desire to prove themselves. While their goal may be to land a prestigious job.

Motivation: What does your main character want more than anything else? How does this become important, necessary, and urgent in the story?

_____
_____
_____
_____
_____
_____
_____

Goal: What is your main character's ultimate goal? How does this goal relate to the main idea or theme of your story?

_____
_____
_____
_____

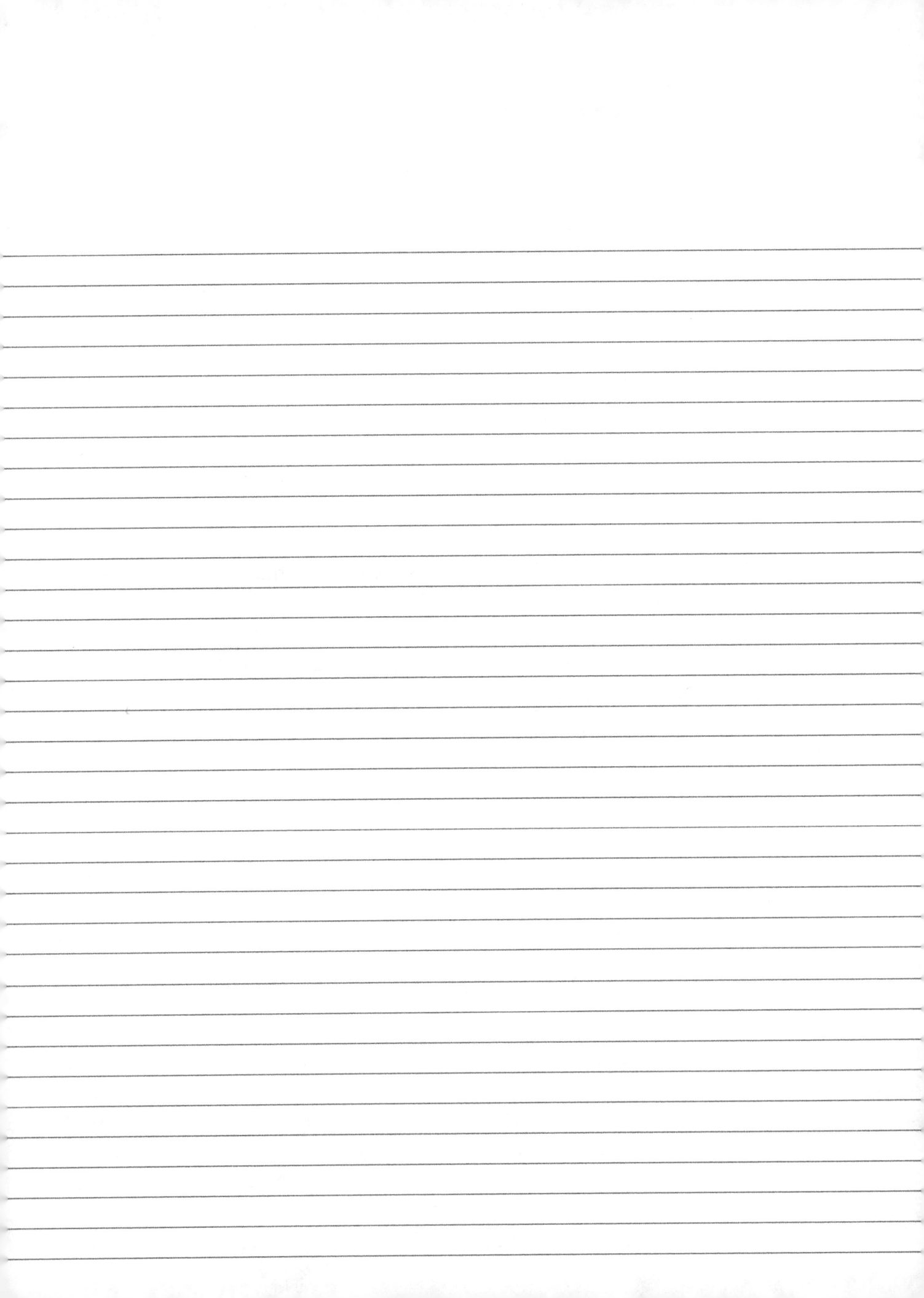

⑨ THE NORMAL

Establishing a normal day for the main character at the beginning of a book serves a couple of important purposes in storytelling.

First, it helps to set the stage by grounding the reader in the story's setting and provides a baseline for what is considered "normal" in the main character's world. This creates a foundation for the reader to understand how the character's world works and what is at stake when things change.

Second, establishing a normal day also helps to develop the main character. By showing the character going about their daily routine, the reader can learn a lot about the character's personality, habits, and relationships. This is important for creating a connection between the reader and the character, as it allows the reader to get to know the character on a deeper level.

By the time the story's events unfold, the reader will have a strong sense of who the main character is and can better understand the significance of the story's events.

Describe a typical day in your main character's life. Include their introduction into the story in a way that reveals their essential character. By highlighting the main character's unique qualities, actions, or thoughts, the reader can gain a better understanding of who they are and what drives them. Overall, the goal is to make the reader care about the character, even before the main plot begins.

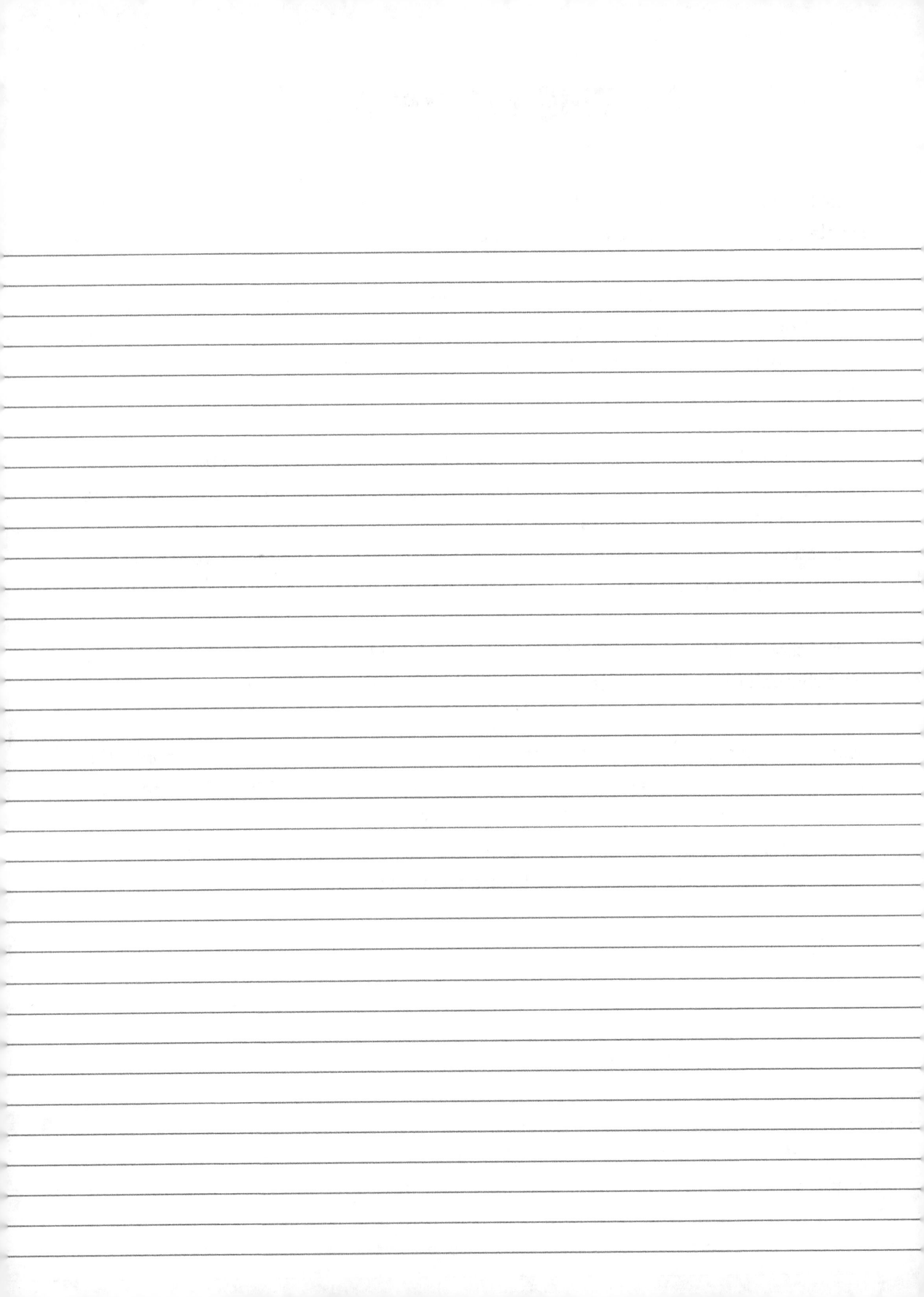

⑩ NEMESIS

A nemesis, or antagonist, provides a crucial opposing force for the protagonist, creating conflict and tension that drives the plot forward.

A nemesis challenges the protagonist's beliefs and goals, forcing them to grow and evolve as a character. A well-developed nemesis can also add depth and complexity to the story's themes and messages.

Some examples of opposing forces are a rival, villain, nature, societal norms, or a personal flaw within the protagonist.

Who or what opposes your protagonist?

_____
_____
_____
_____
_____
_____
_____
_____
_____
_____
_____

In what ways does this nemesis prevent your main character from achieving their goals?

_____
_____
_____
_____
_____
_____
_____
_____

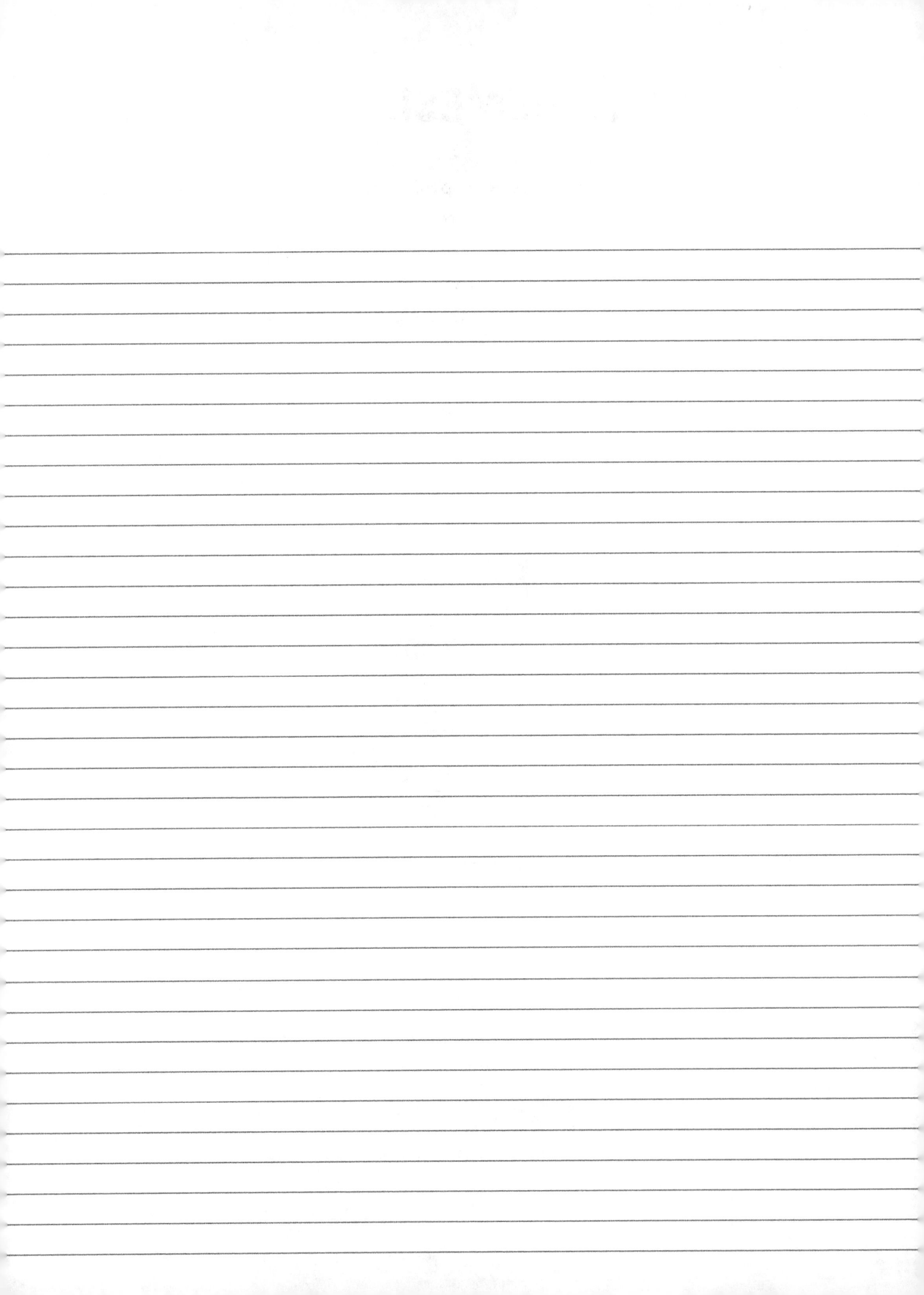

⑪ MAIN CONFLICT

A main conflict provides tension, drama, and a sense of urgency to the narrative. It gives the story direction and purpose, allowing the characters to face challenges and grow as they try to overcome the conflict.

Without a main conflict, a story can feel aimless and lacking in depth, making it difficult to engage the reader. A well-crafted conflict can make a story memorable and impactful.

To create a conflict, establish your protagonist's goal or desire (as we did in lesson #8). Then, introduce an obstacle that prevents the protagonist from achieving their goal.

Here are some examples of main conflicts in a story: person vs person, person vs self, person vs nature, person vs society, and person vs technology.

Make sure the conflict is tied to the theme of your story and has the potential to create tension, suspense, and emotional investment in your reader.

What's the main conflict of your story?

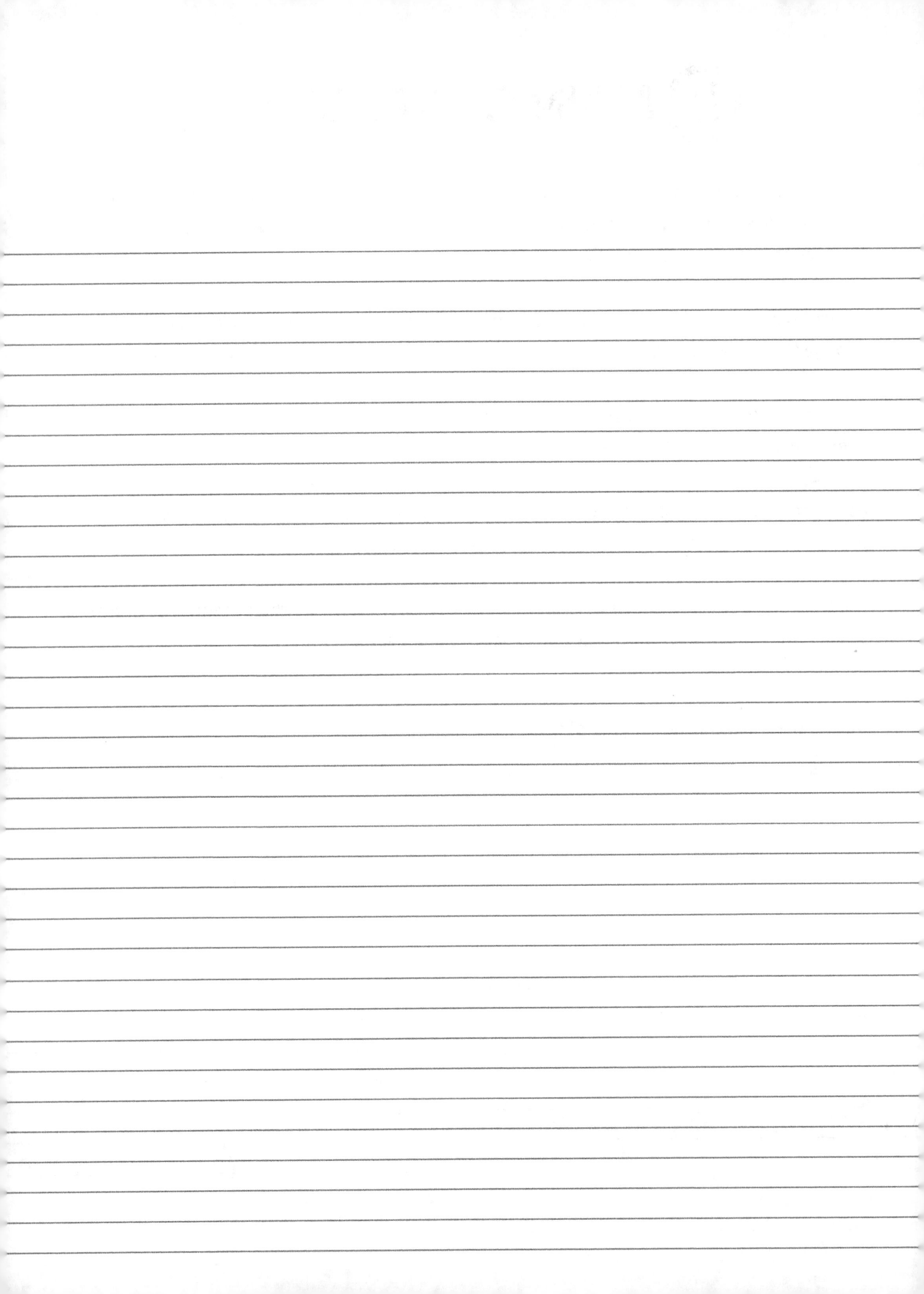

⑫ OBSTACLES

Obstacles create conflict and tension, which makes the story more interesting for readers. They should be significant and challenging, forcing the protagonist to take action and make difficult choices.

Without obstacles, a story can feel flat and lack momentum. They also provide opportunities for character development, as the protagonist must overcome the obstacles and grow in the process.

Some examples of obstacles a protagonist might face in a story are physical, emotional, psychological, time-related, interpersonal, and moral.

How will the obstacles prevent your main character from achieving their goals?

_____
_____
_____
_____
_____
_____
_____
_____
_____
_____
_____

How does the main conflict (from lesson #11) challenge your protagonist and prevent them from achieving their goals?

_____
_____
_____
_____
_____
_____
_____
_____
_____

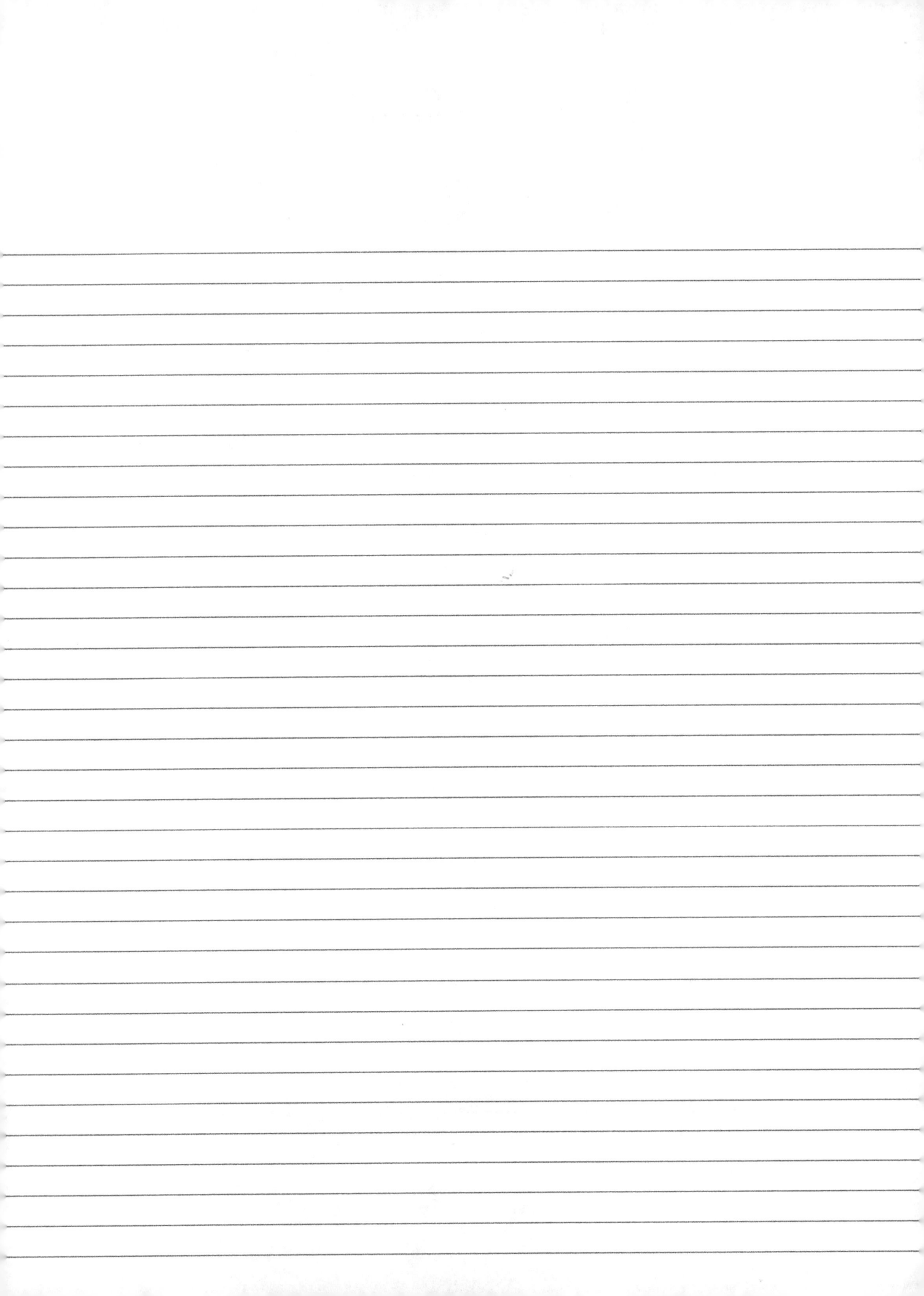

⑬ SUPPORTING CHARACTERS

Supporting characters are your protagonist's friends, acquaintances, family, pets, coworkers, or neighbors. All of them must be relevant to the plot and the story.

Who are your supporting characters? Select one memorable characteristic that defines them and makes them unique.

_____

_____

_____

_____

_____

_____

_____

_____

_____

What are their roles and relationships to the protagonist?

_____

_____

_____

_____

_____

_____

_____

_____

_____

_____

_____

_____

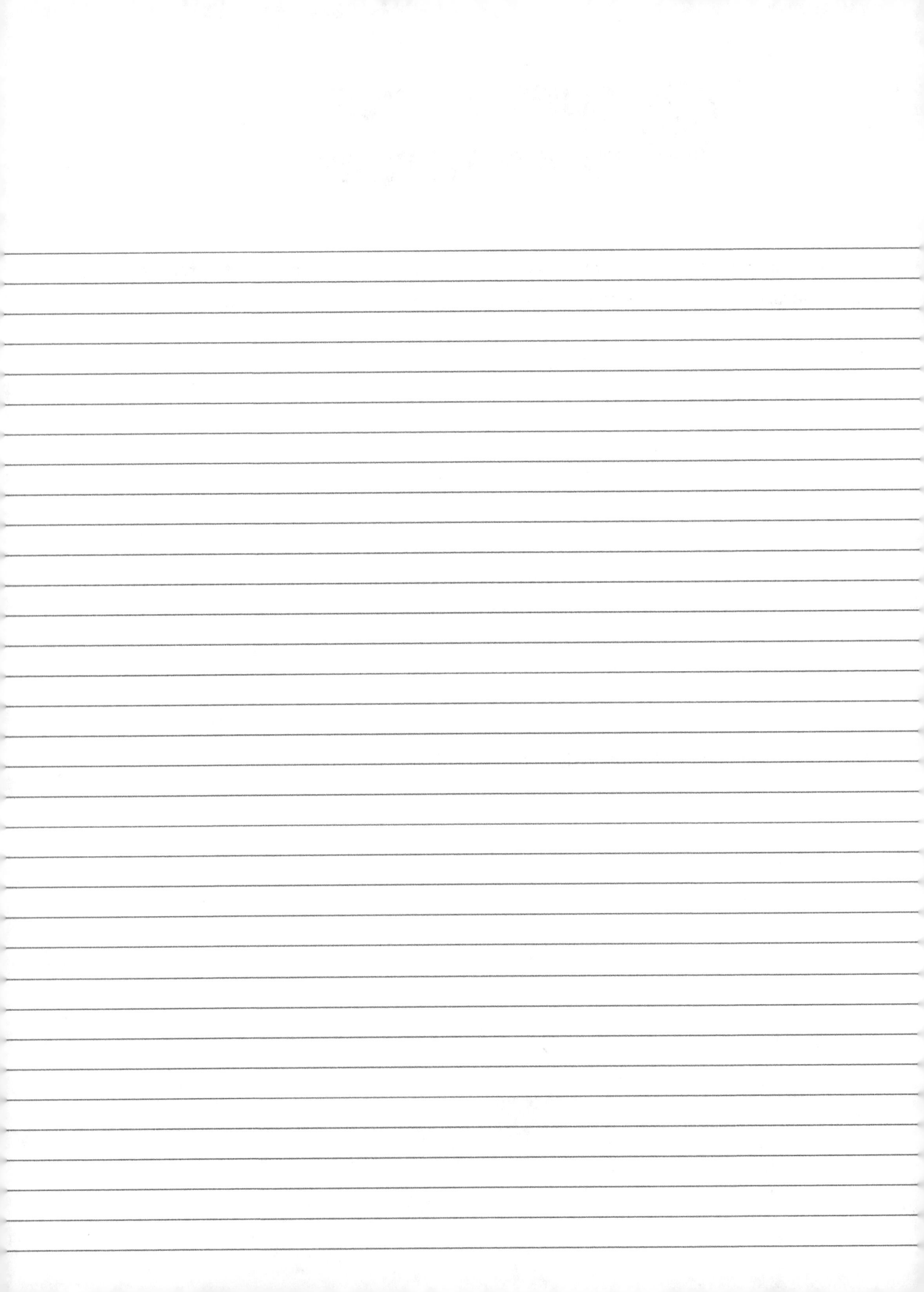

⑭ OPENING SCENE

The opening scene is one of the most critical elements of a story. It's the moment that determines whether a reader will continue reading or set the book aside.

This scene should set the stage for the novel and create an emotional connection between the reader and the protagonist.

To write a great opening scene, remember to keep it exciting and descriptive. Use your words to paint a picture in the reader's mind, so they can imagine what's happening. Try to use all five senses (sight, sound, touch, taste, and smell) to make it even more immersive.

Don't forget to think about what your main character wants or needs, too. This will help you create a hook that will make the reader want to keep reading.

Be careful not to reveal too much information all at once, as it could ruin the unexpected or suspenseful elements that make the story interesting.

With what action will you start your story? Where does your story start? When is it taking place?

(15) INCITING INCIDENT

The inciting incident sets the story's plot into motion.

It should be a clear and defining moment in the protagonist's life that sets them on the path to achieving their objective.

Timing is important, and it should occur early enough to capture the reader's attention but not too soon that character development is sacrificed.

A well-crafted inciting incident should propel the story forward and create a sense of urgency that drives the reader to keep turning the pages.

For example, in "Harry Potter and the Sorcerer's Stone" by J.K. Rowling, the inciting incident occurs when Harry Potter receives a letter informing him he is a wizard and has been accepted to attend Hogwarts School of Witchcraft and Wizardry. This sets off a chain of events that leads Harry on a journey of discovery and adventure.

What event intrudes into your protagonist's normal life that launches this character into the main conflict in your story?

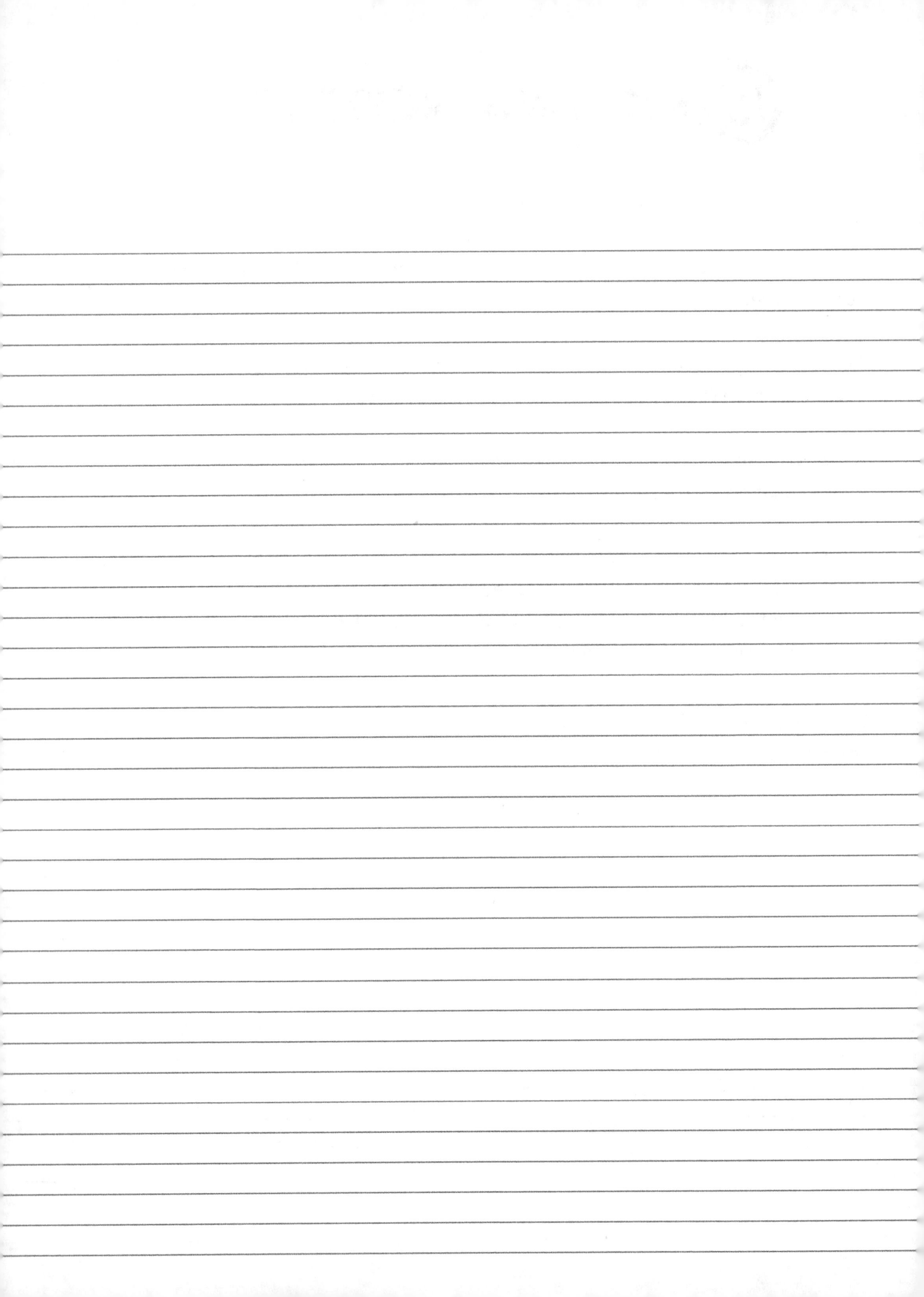

(16) IMPENDING BAD THING

The impending bad thing creates tension and anticipation for the reader.

It's the feeling something terrible is about to happen, which generates suspense and keeps the reader invested in the story. It's a looming "ticking time bomb" that's significant enough to motivate the protagonist and create a sense of urgency.

The impending bad thing can be anything from a natural disaster to an imminent threat from an antagonist, but it must be a clear and present danger the protagonist must face.

Establish the stakes early in the story and make sure the reader understands the potential consequences of failure.

The impending bad thing should be linked to the protagonist's goals, and it should structure the story in a way that builds towards a climactic moment.

What impending bad thing will happen if your main character isn't successful or chooses not to move forward into the story?

_____
_____
_____
_____
_____
_____
_____
_____
_____
_____
_____
_____
_____
_____
_____

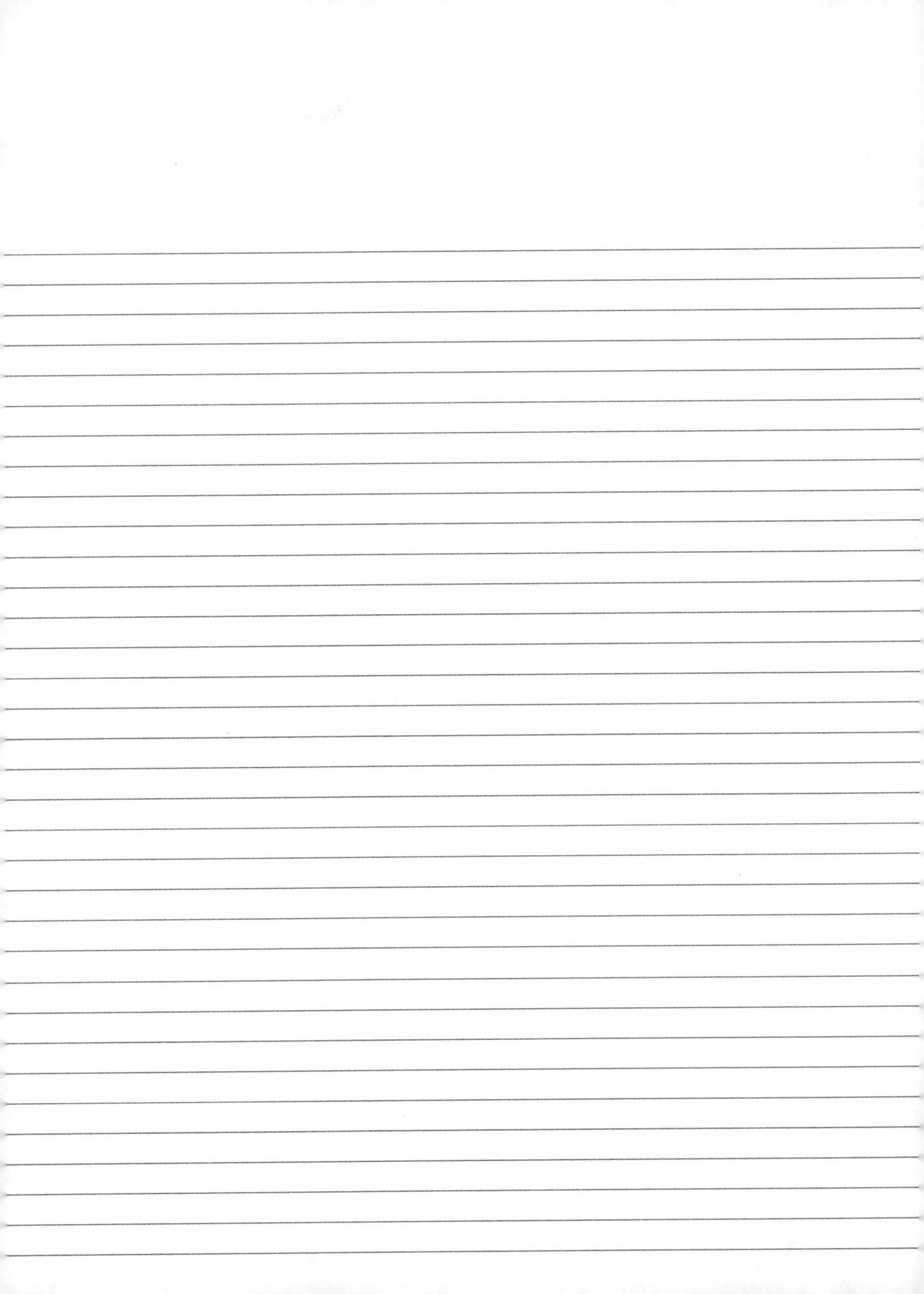

⑰ FORESHADOWING

Foreshadowing is a literary technique that hints at future events, creating a sense of inevitability and heightening the reader's interest in the story.

Foreshadowing should be subtle enough to create intrigue without being too obvious, but also be clear enough for the reader to connect the dots when the events occur.

To create effective foreshadowing, identify key moments in your story and consider how they can be hinted at earlier in the narrative.

Some ways to achieve foreshadowing are through dialogue, setting, and symbolism. It's also essential to ensure the foreshadowing is relevant to the story and it assists in developing the characters and the plot.

By using foreshadowing effectively, you can create a more satisfying reading experience, as the reader will feel more connected to the story and invested in the outcome.

How will you use foreshadowing to create tension and suspense in your story?

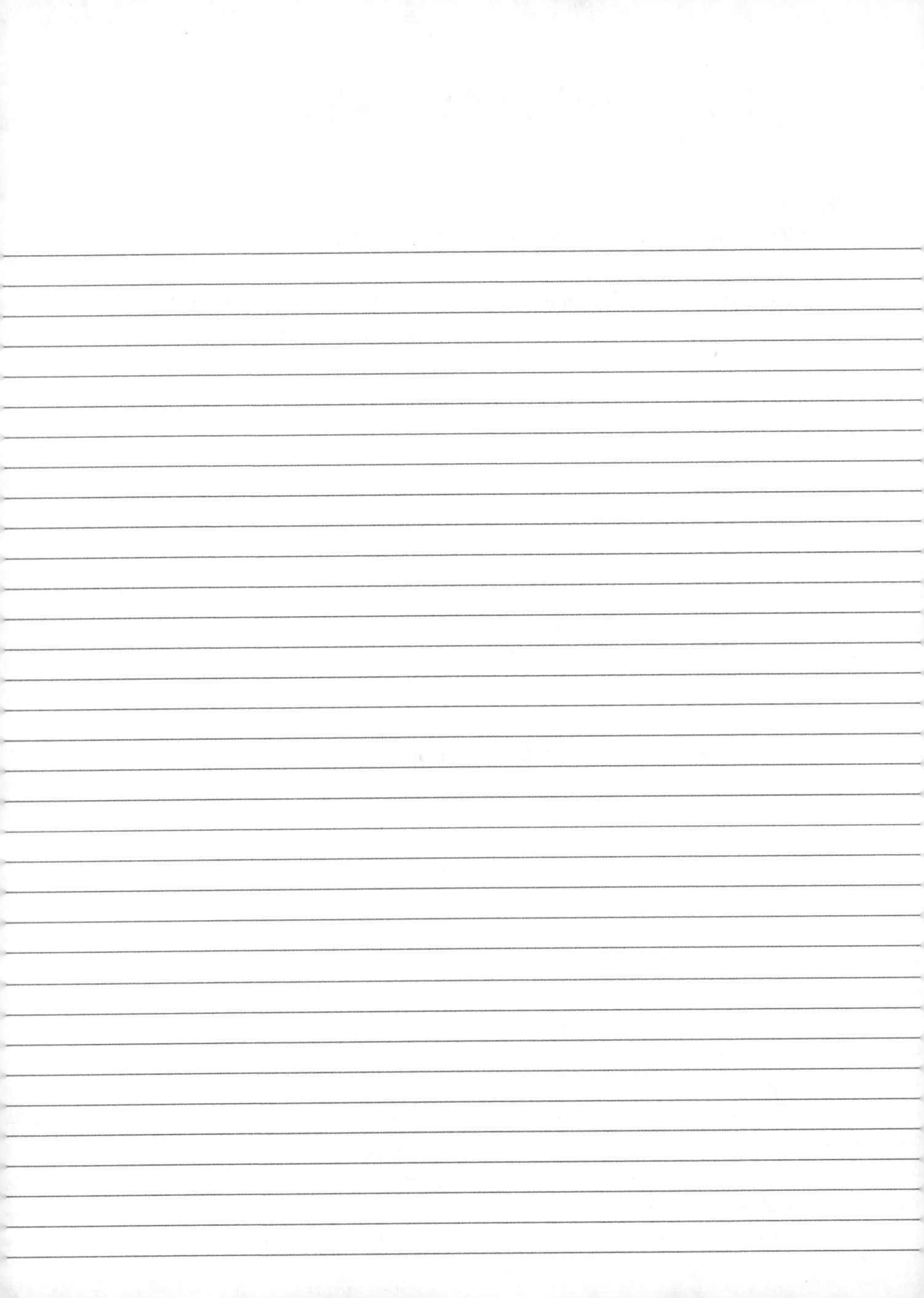

(18) ESCALATION

Escalating events are the gradual increase in tension and conflict that propels the narrative forward and keeps the reader invested in the outcome.

The events should be linked to the protagonist's goals, increase in intensity as the story progresses, and create a sense of momentum that drives the story forward.

To create effective escalating events, consider the pacing of the story, making sure the events occur at the right time to maintain the reader's interest.

The events should be unpredictable enough to keep the reader guessing, but not so outlandish they strain the reader's suspension of disbelief.

By creating escalating events, you keep the reader engaged and eager to know what happens next.

The escalating events should lead to a climactic moment that resolves the central conflict of the story, leaving the reader satisfied and fulfilled.

What series of escalating events build toward a climactic moment in your story? List at least three events and describe how they escalate the conflict and challenge your main character.

⑲ ESCALATION RESPONSE

The main character's response to the escalating events reveals their personality, motivations, and growth throughout the story.

It's important to craft a response that's authentic to the character and moves the story forward.

The response should be logical and believable, and it should reflect the consequences of the escalating events.

It should also be proactive and not reactive, as the main character should drive the story forward, rather than being pushed by external forces.

By creating an interesting response to escalating events, you can deepen the reader's connection to the main character and create a sense of investment in the story's outcome.

How does your main character respond to the escalation events you listed in lesson #18?

(20) ACT ONE

The three-act structure is a common storytelling framework used in literature, film, and theater.

It divides a story into three main sections: the setup, the confrontation, and the resolution.

By using this structure, you can create a coherent and intriguing narrative that builds momentum and maintains the reader's interest throughout the story.

Act one in a novel sets up the story, introducing the characters and setting. It should also introduce the central conflict and establish the stakes, giving the reader a reason to care about what happens next.

What happens in act one of your story? List three plot points.

_____
_____
_____
_____
_____
_____
_____
_____
_____
_____
_____
_____
_____
_____
_____
_____

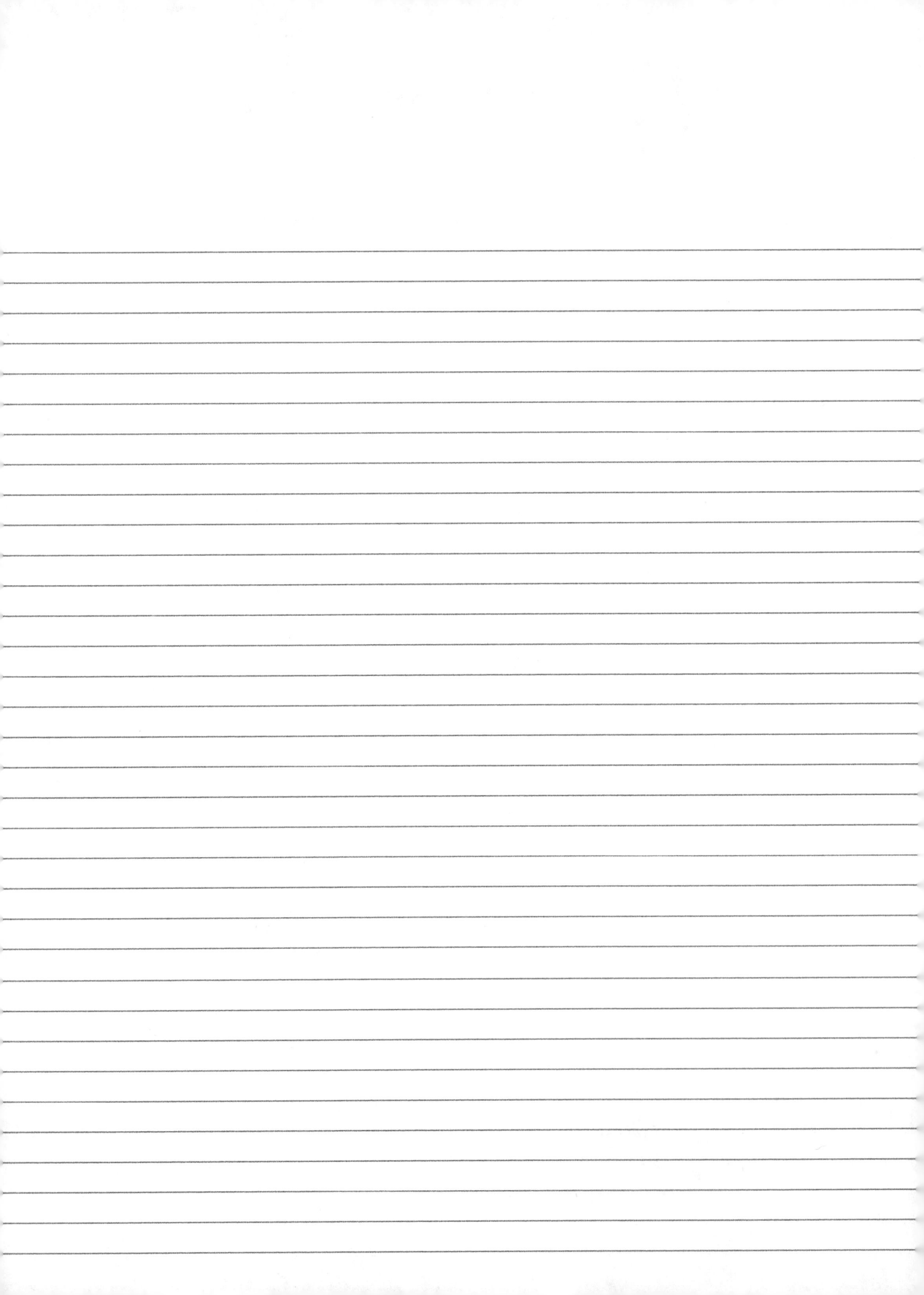

(21) ACT TWO

The second act, also known as the confrontation, comprises the bulk of the story and includes rising tension, conflicts, and obstacles the protagonist must overcome.

Your escalation points and responses are usually woven into your story in this act.

By the end of act two, the main character should be at their lowest point, facing a seemingly insurmountable challenge that sets up the climatic moment in act three.

Act two should be a rollercoaster of emotions and action, leaving the reader eager to know how the story will end.

What happens in act two of your story? List three plot points.

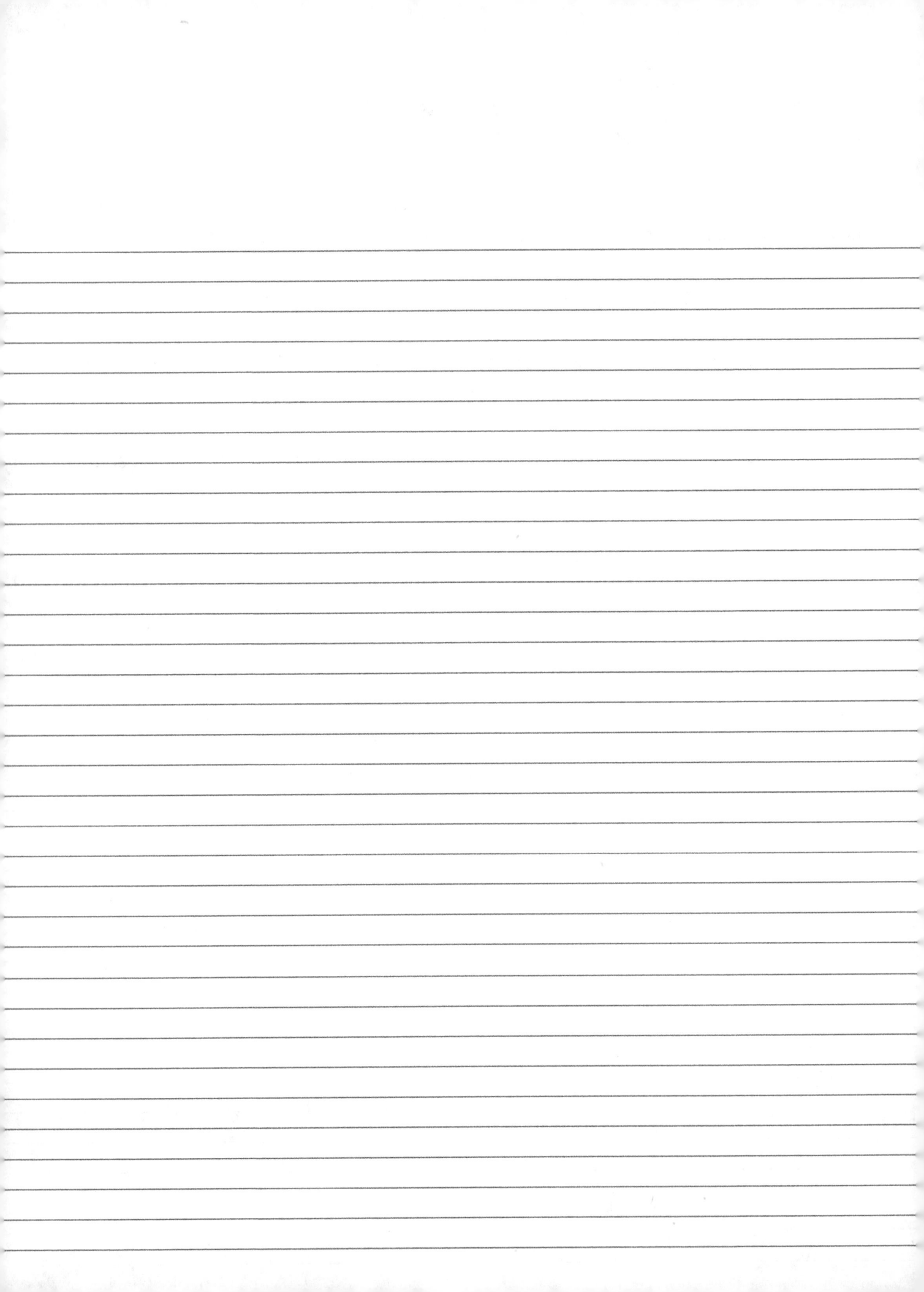

(22) ACT THREE

Act three is the final act. It's the resolution where the protagonist confronts and overcomes the story's main conflict (in the climax, lesson #25), leading to a satisfying conclusion.

Conflicts that have been introduced are resolved and the story's loose ends are tied up, leaving the reader with a sense of closure.

It's essential to have a clear understanding of the resolution of your story and what messages you want to convey to your readers.

The third act should be the most exciting and the most engaging part of the book. It's important to ensure the pacing is correct, and the tension is maintained throughout the act.

Remember to give the reader a conclusion that leaves them feeling content and gratified with the journey they've just completed with your characters.

What happens in act three of your story? List three plot points.

(23) DON'T FORGET THE NEMESIS

You've already decided on the opposing force and plotted your three acts. Now make sure you don't forget to include what the nemesis (from lesson #10) is doing while all this action is going on.

A well-crafted nemesis adds depth and complexity to the story by representing opposing values, beliefs, or motives that clash with those of the protagonist.

By having a nemesis, the stakes of the story are raised, and the tension is increased, making the story more engaging and memorable for the reader.

A nemesis is a vital component of any well-developed fictional story, providing an essential conflict that drives the plot forward and adds depth and complexity to the story.

What's the nemesis doing during the three acts?

(24) MORE SETTINGS

Using different settings can help bring a story to life and create a more immersive experience for the reader.

Settings can create different obstacles and opportunities for the characters to face, which can advance the plot and keep the story moving forward. For example, if the protagonist needs to travel across the ocean to find a magical item, it can create a sense of adventure and challenge.

Incorporating different settings and cultures can make a story more diverse and inclusive, and help readers learn about different people and places.

Settings can also create a sense of contrast, making sure scenes or characters stand out more vividly against a backdrop of other locations. This can help the story feel more dynamic and appealing.

What settings will your characters encounter in the story? List at least three.

(25) CLIMAX

The climax is the point of highest tension when the conflict or main problem of the story reaches its most critical point.

It's the moment when the main character faces their greatest challenge and must make a crucial decision or take action to resolve the conflict.

A successful climax is based on the sense of rising tension and conflict throughout your story that culminates in a final, intense moment of resolution. This moment should be the most emotionally charged and action-packed scene in your book.

For example, the climax of "Harry Potter and the Sorcerer's Stone" is when Harry and his friends face off against Professor Quirrell in the underground chamber where the Sorcerer's Stone is being kept. During the confrontation, Harry realizes he can touch Quirrell without being burned due to the love and protection from his mother's sacrifice. Harry defeats Quirrell and seizes the Stone, saving the day and preventing Voldemort from returning to power.

What causes your main character to reach their breaking point? What decision does your main character make at the climactic moment in the story? Where does this take place (setting)?

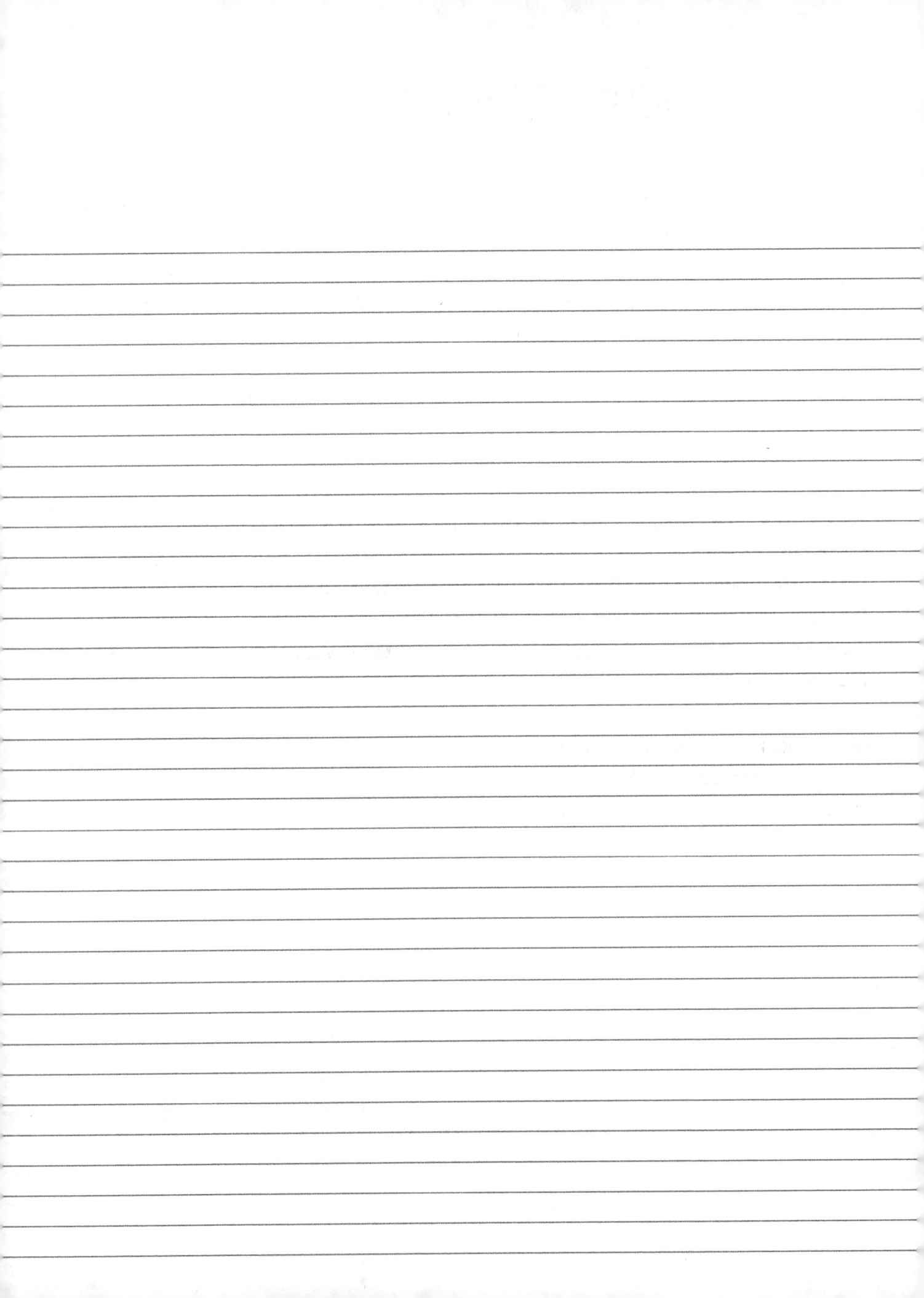

(26) AFTERMATH

The part of the story immediately after the climax is called the aftermath or falling action. This is the point in the story where the tension and conflict resolve, and the story winds down toward the conclusion.

It's important to make sure the falling action flows naturally from the climax, giving readers a chance to catch their breath and reflect on what has just happened.

Use this opportunity to reinforce the themes and messages of your story, providing a deeper understanding of the characters and their journey.

Be careful not to rush through the falling action or add unnecessary information, as this can detract from the satisfying conclusion you've worked so hard to create.

The falling action of "Harry Potter and the Sorcerer's Stone" happens when Harry and his friends return to Hogwarts and are praised for their heroism. Dumbledore explains to Harry that the Stone has been destroyed, ensuring that Voldemort cannot return using it.

What does your main character do immediately after making their decision in the climax?

_____
_____
_____
_____
_____
_____
_____
_____
_____
_____
_____
_____
_____

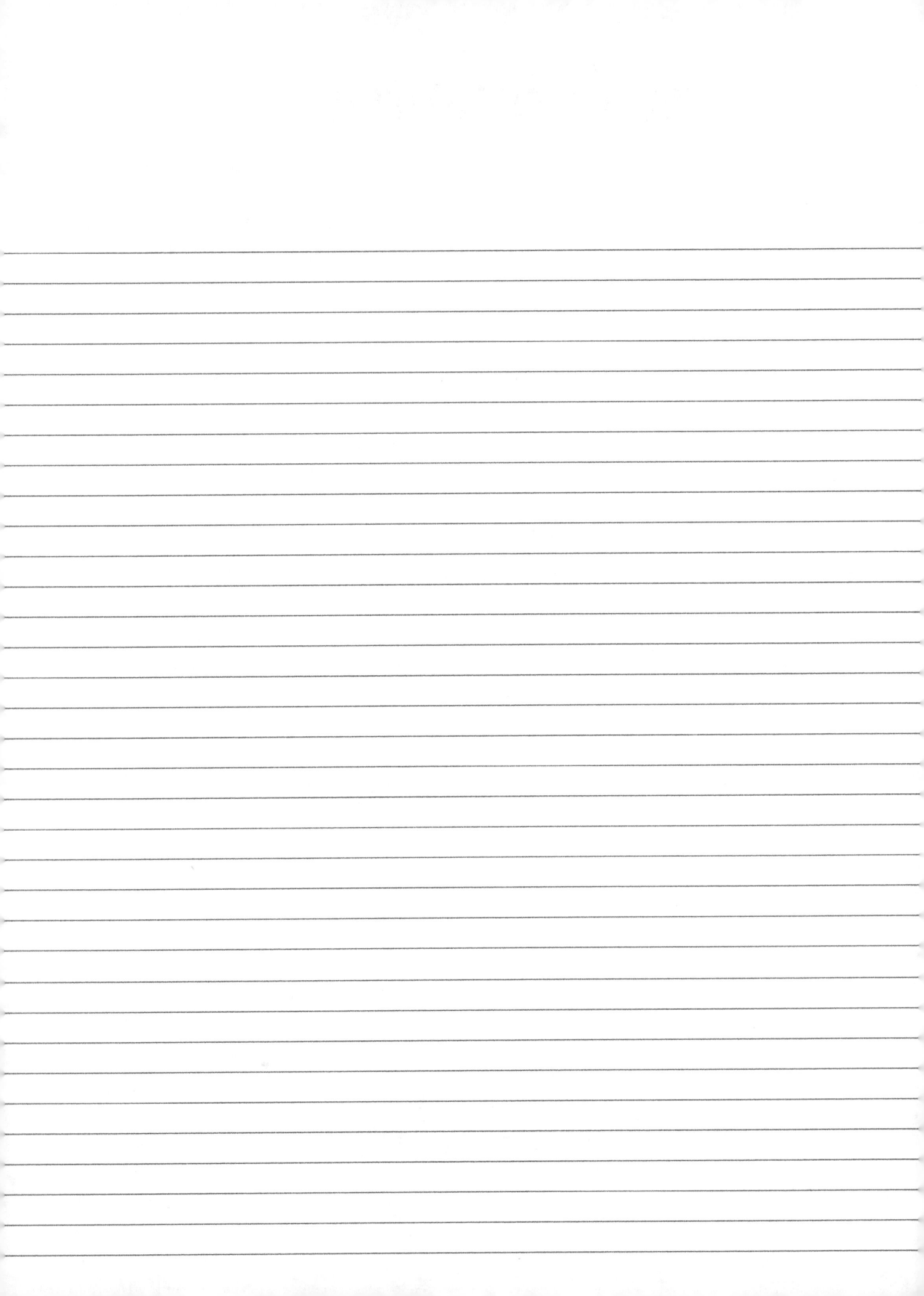

(27) CONCLUSION

The conclusion of a novel is the final part of the story that ties up loose ends and resolves the main conflict, often showing the protagonist's growth.

It should provide closure for the reader and reflect on the themes and messages of the story, leaving the reader with a sense of satisfaction and a clear understanding of the resolution.

This can be achieved by showing how the protagonist's actions or decisions have led to a greater understanding or acceptance of a particular idea or concept.

At the conclusion of "Harry Potter and the Sorcerer's Stone," Harry and his friends board the Hogwarts Express to return home for the summer, but their friendship remains strong. Harry feels a sense of belonging and excitement for the next school year, and the story ends on a hopeful note, setting up the events of the rest of the series. This scene provides closure and sets up the resolution of the story while leading into the events of the next book.

How did your protagonist resolve their main conflict? How did they come to make their choice in the climax? Where does your story's conclusion take place (setting)?

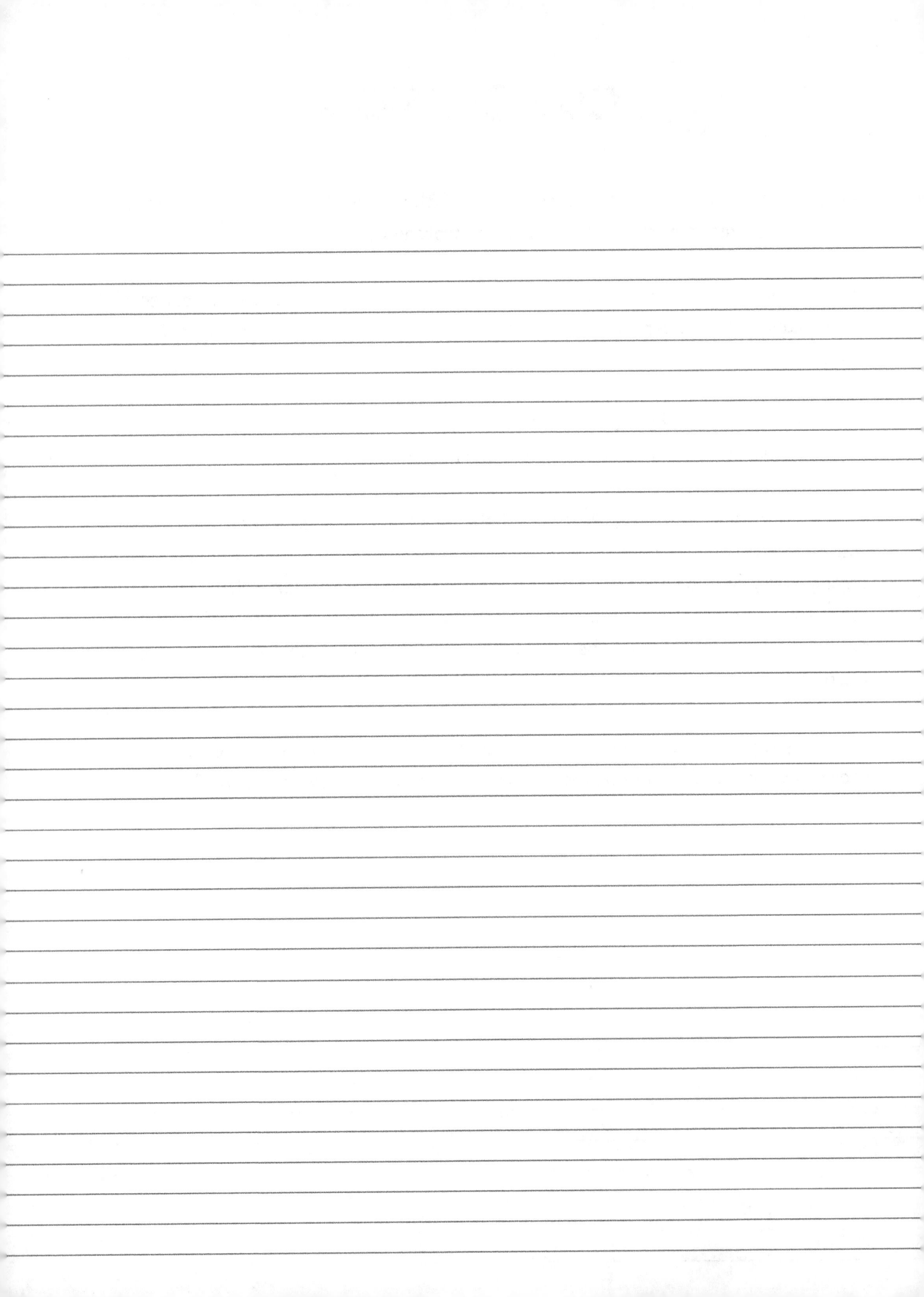

(28) REWARD & CONSEQUENCE

A story's reward and consequence provide closure and satisfaction to readers.

The reward results from the main character's actions, while the consequence arises from their mistakes or missteps.

This approach creates a memorable and realistic conclusion, reminding the reader of the story's stakes.

In "Harry Potter and the Sorcerer's Stone," the main character's reward is multifaceted, including the prevention of Voldemort's victory, increased popularity and respect, and the opportunity for Harry to attend Hogwarts.

However, the consequence of the main character's actions is the danger Harry faces in preventing Voldemort from obtaining the Sorcerer's Stone. Harry and his friends are in constant danger of being discovered and thwarted by Voldemort's followers. Ultimately, Harry risks his own life to defeat Voldemort and learns that he has a dangerous enemy who will stop at nothing to gain power and destroy his enemies.

What reward does your protagonist get for making their choice? What consequences do they suffer?

(29) FINAL STATE

The protagonist's final state is their condition after they've completed their journey and achieved their goal.

Their decision at the climax has left the main character a changed person. Show how the protagonist has overcome their flaws or weaknesses and how they've learned from their experiences.

During this time of reflection, the protagonist contemplates the valuable lessons and transformations they've experienced, gaining insight into how they can apply these lessons to improve their daily life.

For example, in "Harry Potter and the Sorcerer's Stone," Harry is happy and relieved after the defeat of Voldemort and the prevention of him obtaining the Sorcerer's Stone. He also feels a sense of belonging and excitement for the next school year, as he has made friends and discovered a new world of magic. Harry is optimistic and hopeful about the future.

What's your main character like now after their journey? How has your main character grown and changed?

(30) LINGERING DANGER

Implying a hint of danger still exists at the end of your book can create tension and uncertainty, making the story memorable.

It can also help to create a sense of realism in the story. In real life, not all conflicts can be resolved completely, and there may still be some risks or uncertainties that linger even after the main problem has been handled.

Hinting at a lingering danger can also set the stage for a sequel or follow-up story. By leaving some loose ends or unresolved conflicts, you can create the potential for a new adventure or continuation of the story.

At the end of "Harry Potter and the Sorcerer's Stone," Dumbledore warns that while Voldemort may've been defeated for the time being, he will return. Additionally, Hagrid lets slip that Harry's parents didn't die in a car crash as he previously believed, hinting at a darker truth that will be explored in the subsequent books.

What hint of danger still exists in your story?

(31) TITLE

A good title can help your book stand out from the crowd, communicate the genre of your book, and create interest in your story. Here are some tips to help you create a catchy title.

Keep the title simple and memorable. A good title should be easy to remember and easy to spell.

Consider your book's genre. Your title should give readers an idea of what your story is about and reflect the genre of your book.

Use keywords. Using keywords in your title can make your book easier to find online and can also help potential readers understand what your book is about.

Avoid clichés. While clichés can be tempting, they can also make your title sound generic and unoriginal. Try to come up with something that's unique and memorable.

Test it out. Once you have a few potential titles, test them out on friends, family, or even online communities to see which ones resonate the most with people.

A good title can make a big difference in the success of your book. It can attract readers, create interest, and set the tone for your story.

Take the time to brainstorm and test out different options until you find the perfect title for your book.

Brainstorm your title ideas here:

_____
_____
_____
_____
_____
_____
_____
_____
_____

EXTRA CREDIT

Write a one-page (300-word) synopsis for your story.

A synopsis summarizes the main plot, characters, themes, and conflict of a novel in a concise manner.

It provides an overview of the story's events, setting, and the protagonist's journey while leaving out minor details.

Writing a brief synopsis before beginning the actual writing process can be beneficial in clarifying the plot, themes, and character arcs (the transformation or development of a character throughout a story), serving as a roadmap for you to stay focused and on track.

It can also attract interest from agents, editors, publishers, or potential readers, and can be used to test the concept of your book.

_____
_____
_____
_____
_____
_____
_____
_____
_____
_____
_____
_____
_____
_____
_____
_____
_____
_____
_____
_____
_____
_____
_____
_____

Write "Congratulations" here:

_____

Pat yourself on the back, you've finished this workbook!

Now take this outline and write your story!

Congrats

WRITING TIPS

1. Omit unnecessary words. Look for words that can be cut without changing the sentence's meaning. The top five worst offenders are: very, actually, that, just, really. Make every word count.

2. Avoid using cliches. Keep the writing fresh and original.

3. Watch your tenses. Don't start in the present tense and end in the past tense.

4. Create smooth transitions. Use traditional phrases, or your story will be choppy.

5. Don't go overboard with descriptions. Use descriptions necessary to the story and let readers use their imagination.

6. Subtly convey important messages throughout the story without preaching.

7. Show readers, don't tell. Visualize each scene.

8. Begin your story when the action starts. Use this to show emotion, thoughts, and feelings without turning it into a direct statement.

9. Don't write dialogue exactly as it is spoken. For example, avoid using words like "gonna" instead of "going to" unless it helps define the character's personality.

10. Each scene should tie into the plot and move the story forward.

11. Use active voice as much as possible. Passive voice tells the reader what happened. Active voice shows the reader the action.

WRITING TIPS CONTINUED

12. Stay away from using coincidences to propel your story forward. Events grow out of characters' actions and the clashing of their desires.

13. Keep the use of adverbs to a minimum. These often weaken the impact of the verb.

14. Create conflict or obstacles that challenge the protagonist and force them to make choices that move the story forward.

15. Network with other writers. Connect with other writers through writing groups, social media, and online forums. Build a community of writers who can offer support and advice.

16. Attend writing conferences and workshops to learn more about the craft of writing and to connect with other authors.

17. Use beta readers to get feedback on your story. A beta reader reads a written work, such as a manuscript, before publication to provide feedback to the author. Ask for constructive criticism and take it into account when revising your work.

18. Continue to write and improve your craft. The more you write, the better you'll become.

19. Keep learning and growing. Never stop learning and growing as a writer. Read widely, take classes, and continue to challenge yourself. Writing is a lifelong journey, and the more you put into it, the more you'll get out of it.

20. Writing is a process. It's okay if your first draft isn't perfect. Revising and editing are important parts of crafting a great story.

Be the first to get updates about D.L. Armillei & Your Fantasy Portal

by signing up for my newsletters at:

www.YourFantasyPortal.com

www.DLArmillei.com

Keep in touch by checking out my social media:

Your Fantasy Portal on YouTube

@YourFantasyPortal
on TikTok, Pinterest, Facebook Page, and Instagram

@DLArmillei
on Twitter, Facebook Page, Instagram

D. L. Armillei Author links:

BookBub
https://www.bookbub.com/profile/d-l-armillei

Goodreads
https://www.goodreads.com/DLArmillei

Amazon
https://www.amazon.com/D.-L.-Armillei/e/BO6XD25WT4/

Also by D. L. Armillei

Shock of Fate *Book One Anchoress Series*

Plague of Death *Book Two Anchoress Series*

Helm of Awe *Book Three Anchoress Series*

Hag's Hut on the Hill - a Short Story/Deleted Scene from the Anchoress Series (newsletter sign-up)

www.ingramcontent.com/pod-product-compliance
Lightning Source LLC
Chambersburg PA
CBHW080527030426
42337CB00023B/4652